# BLUES PICTURE CHORDS AND HOW TO USE THEM.

*By Happy Traum.*

Order No. AM 21676
International Standard Book Number: 0.8256.2186.0

*Exclusive Distributors:*
Music Sales Corporation
257 Park Avenue South, New York, NY 10010
Music Sales Limited
8/9 Frith Street, London W1V 5TZ England
Music Sales Pty. Limited
120 Rothschild Street, Rosebery, Sydney, NSW 2018, Australia

Printed in the United States of America by
Vicks Lithograph and Printing Corporation

# Introduction

This book is designed to teach you, in a clear way, the chords and progressions you will need to play songs in the blues form. Through the use of pictures and diagrams, the basic chords in each key become easily recognized and immediately useful.

*Blues Picture Chords* can be used as a step-by-step learning method, as a chord reference book, or as a practice guide to help strengthen your chord technique. Some blues songs have been added for both their interest and for practical application of the chords shown.

For best results, the beginner should proceed systematically, making sure he plays all the practice progressions and memorizes every chord, playing them until they can be fretted accurately and quickly. Once the chords in a particular key are learned thoroughly, they should be applied to these and other blues songs. There are many excellent blues songbooks on the market for further investigation of this fascinating field of music, and the student is encouraged to learn as many songs from books and records as he or she can.

*Blues Picture Chords* starts with the simplest first position chords, but progresses quickly to more complex positions, including bar chords and other movable patterns. This book will not only be useful in playing blues, but can increase your knowledge and technique for any kind of music, whether jazz, folk, rock or pop.

How to hold the guitar

# Chord Diagrams

The chord diagram is a picture, or a map, of the guitar fingerboard. Six vertical lines represent the six strings, and the shorter, horizontal lines represent the frets. Circles indicate the place at which the string is fretted, and the number within the circle indicates the finger of the left hand to be used. Each diagram is drawn as if the guitar were facing you, in a vertical position. Therefore, the sixth, or bass string, is on the left, and the first (the thinnest) is on the right.

An X next to a string indicates that the string is not strummed or picked with that particular chord. If there is no mark over the string, that string is played *open*, and is not fretted by the left hand.

# The Right Hand

Blues can be played either with a flatpick or with the fingers, depending on the kind of sound you want to get. A country blues guitarist will invariably play in a finger style, using the thumb on the bass notes while the fingers pick out the treble melody notes. A more modern player would tend to strum the chords with a flatpick in the manner of a jazz guitarist. This book is designed to teach you as many useful chords as possible, but I have also provided suggestions in tablature for both pick and finger style blues guitar patterns.

When playing the rhythms notated in this book, a slash mark **/** represents a one-beat strum across the strings of the guitar in a downward direction. A double slash mark **//** means that you strum an eighth note rhythm using a down-up stroke. These are included to give you an idea of the rhythmic possibilities in blues playing, and may be varied and improvised as much as you'd like.

3

# Key of E

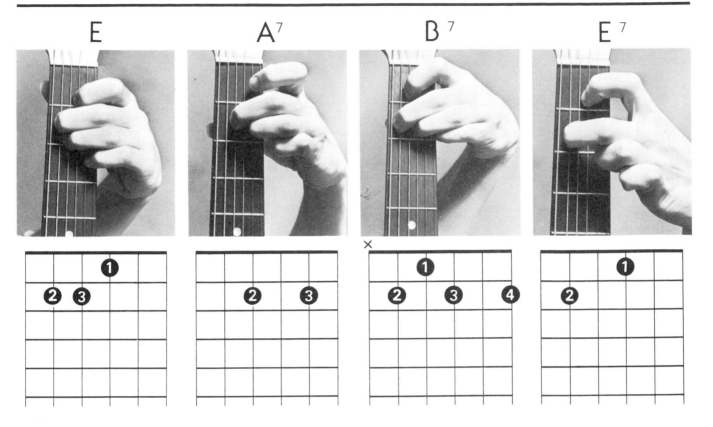

## Checkpoints

—Play each note with the tip of your finger so as not to touch the neighboring strings.

—Your fingers may become sore at first, but they will develop callouses and toughen up before long.

—Notice that in the E and B7 chords, your second finger remains in the same position. This will help when changing from one chord to the other.

## 12-Bar Blues Progression in E

# Right Hand: Blues Strum #1

Thumb picks a bass note.
Index and middle fingers brush lightly down, then
up, across the top three or four strings.

# 8-Bar Blues in E

# Key to the Highway

words & music by Big Bill Broonzy and Charles Segar

I got the key    to    the    high - way,___

Lord, I'm bound    to    go.    I'm gon - na    leave here    run - nin'___

cause walk - in's    much __    too    slow. _____

# Key of A

A       D7       E7       A7

### Checkpoints

—Do not strum the 6th string while fretting D7.

—The E7 and A7 chords are different from those shown on page 4. They can be played interchangeably, but each version of the chord has a distinctive sound. Play both versions to hear the difference.

—The A7 noted above utilizes a bar, in which your index finger plays four strings at the same fret. Keep your index finger straight and apply pressure with your thumb behind the neck so that you can fret all four strings evenly.

## 12-Bar Blues Progression in A

# Right Hand: Blues Strum #2

Thumb picks a bass note.
Index and middle fingers brush lightly up-down-up
across the top three or four strings.
The rhythm has a bounce to it, accenting the bass
and down-strokes.

# 8-Bar Blues in A

# Matchbox Blues

Up on the riv - er, Ma - ma, walk down_ by _____ the sea._

_____ Up on the riv - er _____

walk down by _____ the sea._____ I got those

tad - poles and min - nows_ all in_ o - ver_ me._____

# Key of D

### Checkpoints

—Do not strum the 6th string with the D or D7 chords.

—Be sure you press the string close to the fret to prevent it from buzzing. This is especially important with G7.

## 12-Bar Blues Progression in D

# Right Hand: Blues Arpeggio #1

Thumb picks a bass note.
Index finger picks the 3rd string.
Middle and ring fingers pick the 2nd and 1st strings
together.
Index finger picks the 3rd string.

Key of
**D**

# 8-Bar Blues in D

# The Blues Ain't Nothin'

Well the blues ain't _ no - thin', no, the blues ain't_ no - thin'_ but a

good man _ feel - in'_ bad._ No, the blues ain't_ no thin' but a

good man feel - in'_____ bad.

must have _ been _ those wear- y _ blues_ I had._____

9

# Key of G

## Checkpoints

—Do not play the 6th string with the C7 chord.

—If you are having trouble reaching all the notes in the G chord, try arching your wrist forward a little to bring your fingers closer to the fingerboard.

—Notice that in changing from G to G7, you don't have to move your second and third fingers.

## 12-Bar Blues Progression in G

# Right Hand: Combining Blues Strums #1 and #2

Thumb picks a bass note.
Index and middle fingers brush down across the
top strings.
Thumb picks a bass note.
Index and middle fingers brush up-down-up.

Key of G

# 8-Bar Blues in G

# Step It Up and Go

Used to have a gal, she was lit-tle and low. She used to love me but she

don't no more. She had to step it up and go,_____

step it up and go. She could-n't stay there, I de-

clare, she had to step it up and go.

# Key of C

C          F⁷          G⁷          C⁷

## Checkpoints

—Do not play the 5th or 6th strings with F7.

—This version of F7 is a bar chord. Make sure your index finger is straight and applying even pressure to all strings.

## 12-Bar Blues Progression in C

# Right Hand: Blues Fingerpicking Pattern #1

Thumb picks a bass note.
Thumb, index and middle fingers pick the 3rd, 2nd
and 1st strings simultaneously.
Thumb picks a bass note.
Index finger picks the 2nd string.
Thumb picks the 3rd string.
Middle finger picks the 1st string.

Key of C

## 8-Bar Blues in C

## Frankie and Johnny

Frank-ie and John-ny were lov-ers,— Lord-y, how they— could love. Swore to be true— to each oth-er,— just as true as the stars a-bove, He was her man,— but he— done her wrong.—

13

# Key of Em

## Em

## Am

## B⁷

---

### Checkpoints

—When playing B7, make sure your third finger is not muffling the 2nd string.

—Do not play the open 6th string with B7.

---

## 8-Bar Blues Progression in Em

# Right Hand: Blues Arpeggio #2

Thumb picks a bass note.
Index finger picks the 3rd string.
Middle finger picks the 2nd string.
Ring finger picks the 1st string.

Key of
**Em**

# Darlin'

If I'd __ a known my cap-tain was blind, ____ Dar-lin'. __

__ If I'd __ a known my cap-tain was blind, Dar-lin'. __

If I'd __ a known my cap-tain was blind, I would-n't have been to work un-til

half ___ past nine, ____ Dar-lin'. __

15

# Key of Am

## Am

## Dm

## E⁷

---

### Checkpoints

—Do not strum the 6th string with D7.

—Be sure that in the E7 chord your fourth finger stretches out to the 2nd string, third fret.

—When playing Dm, your third finger is lifted up out of the way of the strings.

## 8-Bar Blues Progressions in Am

16

# Right Hand: Blues Arpeggio #3

Thumb picks a bass note.
Index, middle and ring fingers pick the 3rd, 2nd
and 1st strings simultaneously.
Thumb picks a bass note.
Index, middle and ring fingers pick the 3rd, 2nd
and 1st strings separately.

# Saint James Infirmary

It was down in old Joe's Bar - room __ on a
cor - ner __ by the square. The __ drinks were served as
u - sual __ and the u - su - al crowd __ was there.

# The Blues Form

As you have seen by now, most blues songs follow the same basic chord progression, usually a 12- or 8-bar pattern. Although there is some variation of chords within this structure, the basic form remains constant. Once you are thoroughly familiar with the blues form, you can play just about any blues song or instrumental, which is why the blues is a favorite progression when musicians get together to jam.

The most common blues form is the 12-bar progression, which utilizes the three most basic chords in any given key; the tonic (I), the sub-dominant (IV) and the dominant seventh (V7). Usually, the sub-dominant is played as a seventh chord with a more typical blues sound, so I have given them to you this way throughout the book.

Here are the basic chords in the five most widely used keys:

| Key | Tonic (I) | Sub-dominant (IV7) | Dominant 7 (V7) |
|-----|-----------|--------------------|------------------|
| A | A | D7 | E7 |
| C | C | F7 | G7 |
| D | D | G7 | A7 |
| E | E | A7 | B7 |
| G | G | C7 | D7 |

## Other Blues Progressions

The following chord progressions are somewhat more complex than the standard 12- or 8-bar blues that we have been playing up to now. Practice these until they can be played without hesitation.

**Key of C**

**Key of G**

**Key of E**

**Key of A**

**Key of D**

**Blues Form**

# Stagolee

Well I was stand - in' ___ on the cor - ner ___ when I heard my bull - dog _ bark. He was bark - in' at the two men who were gam - blin' in the ___ dark.

19

# Bar Chords

These chords can be moved to any position on the
fingerboard, enabling you to play blues in any key.

## E Position

Major: F          Seventh: F⁷          Minor: Fm

Optional

---

### Checkpoints

—Keep your index finger straight, using your thumb to apply the necessary pressure to the strings.
  Pay special attention to the tone of the 1st, 2nd, and 6th strings.

—Each fret raises the chord by ½ step. Therefore, the E position with the bar on the second fret is
  F♯ ; on the third fret it is G, and so on.

---

Here is a chart of the chords in this position:

| Fret | Major | Seventh | Minor |
|------|-------|---------|-------|
| 2nd | F♯/G♭ | F♯7/G♭7 | F♯m/G♭m |
| 3rd | G | G7 | Gm |
| 4th | G♯/A♭ | G♯7/A♭7 | G♯m/A♭m |
| 5th | A | A7 | Am |
| 6th | A♯/B♭ | A♯/B♭7 | A♯m/B♭m |
| 7th | B | B7 | Bm |
| 8th | C | C7 | Cm |

# Right Hand: Strum with Moving Bass, Barred F Position

Thumb picks a bass note.
Index finger brushes up across the top two or three strings.

Try this with different positions on the fingerboard, using the barred F position.

**Barred F Position**

# New Stranger Blues

I'm a stran - ger here, just blowed _ in your _ town. _____ I'm a stran - ger here, Just blowed in your town. _____ Just be - cause I'm a stran-ger ev - ry - bo - dy wants to dog me _ a - round.

**Bar Chords**

# A Position

| Major: | Seventh: | Minor: |
|--------|----------|--------|
| A♯/B♭ | A♯⁷/B♭⁷ | A♯m/B♭m |

## Checkpoints

—Be sure your index finger is barring the strings accurately. Listen to the 1st, 5th, and 6th to see if they are fretting clearly.

—Be especially careful that you can hear the 3rd string when playing the seventh position.

—As in the E position chords, each fret raises the chord by ½ step. Here is a chart of the chords in this position:

Here is a chart of the chords in this position.

| Fret | Major | Seventh | Minor |
|------|-------|---------|-------|
| 2nd | B | B7 | Bm |
| 3rd | C | C7 | Cm |
| 4th | C♯/D♭ | C♯7/D♭7 | C♯m/D♭m |
| 5th | D | D7 | Dm |
| 6th | D♯/E♭ | D♯7/E♭7 | D♯m/E♭m |
| 7th | E | E7 | Em |
| 8th | F | F7 | Fm |

# Right Hand: Strum with Moving Bass, Barred A Position

Thumb picks a bass note.
Index finger brushes up across the top two or three
strings.

## 12-Bar Blues in A♭

## Sportin' Life Blues

I got a let-ter___ from my home. Most of my

friends are ___ dead and gone. That old night life,___ that old

sport-in' life is kill-in' me. _____

# Movable Seventh Chords

In these positions it will be necessary to damp the open strings (prevent them from sounding) by touching them lightly with the left hand while fretting the notes you need.

## Position One: movable C⁷ | Position Two: movable B⁷ | Position Three: movable F⁷

### Checkpoints

—In the C7 position, damp the 5th string with your third finger and the 1st string with your first finger.

—In the B7 position, damp the 5th string with your second finger and the 2nd string with your third finger.

—In the F7 position, the 5th string is damped by your first finger, and the 1st string by your third finger.

—As with the bar chords, each fret represents ½ step. Therefore, moving the C7 position up the neck would give you C♯7/D♭7, D7, D♯7/E♭7, and so on.

## Blues Progression with Seventh Chords

# Right Hand: Blues Strum #3

Index finger brushes up across the high strings.
Index (and middle) finger brushes down.
Index finger brushes up.
Index (and middle) finger brushes down, followed by a quick damping of the strings with the open hand.

# The 2:19 Train

I'm gon - na    lay    my    head    on some    lone - some    rail - road    line,    and let that    two nine - teen    pa - ci - fy my wor - ried    mind.

# Diminished Chords

The Diminished Chords are indicated by (—) or (dim.) after the chord letter. They are named after any note of the chord.

A –, C –, D♯–/E♭–, F♯–/G♭–    A♯–/B♭–, C♯–/D♭–, E –, G –    B –, D –, F –, G♯–/A♭–

### Checkpoints

—You can move these diminished chords up the neck as long as you do not play the 5th or 6th strings.

—The chords repeat in a new inversion every three frets.

## Practice Progressions

# Right Hand: Blues Fingerpicking Pattern #2

Thumb picks a bass note and the middle finger
picks the 1st string at the same time.
Index finger picks the 2nd string.
Thumb picks the 3rd string.
Middle Finger picks the 1st string.
Thumb picks a bass note.
Index finger picks the 2nd string.
Thumb picks the 3rd string.

# Make Me a Pallet on Your Floor

Make me a pal - let on your floor;_____

make me a pal - let on your floor._____ Make it

soft, make it low, so my good gal won't know.

Make me a pal - let on your floor._____

**Dimin-ished**

# Movable Chords on the High Strings

These chord positions can be used very effectively for playing melodic breaks or harmonies while singing or accompanying other instruments. It is only necessary to avoid or damp the bass strings when they do not fit in the chord you are playing.

| A | A⁷ | D | E⁷ |
|---|----|---|----|

**Fret**

| | | | | |
|---|---|---|---|---|
| 4th fret: | B | B7 | E | F♯7 |
| 5th fret: | C | C7 | F | G7 |
| 7th fret: | D | D7 | G | A7 |
| 9th fret: | E | E7 | A | B7 |

## Practice Progression

28

# Right Hand: Variation on Fingerpicking Pattern #2

Use the A and A7 movable chords on page 28.

# Betty and Dupree

Bet-ty told Du-pree,— I want a dia-mond ring.—

— Yes, Bet-ty told Du-pree,— I want a dia-mond

ring.— Du - pree said to Bet-ty, I'll

get you most a - ny — thing.

# Some Extra Hints for Playing the Blues

## The Turnaround

You have probably noticed that most blues stanzas end with a chord progression that leads your ear back to the beginning of the next verse. This is called the turnaround, and can be played either with chords or melodically. Here are some typical chord turnarounds:

Read the following tablature carefully to play different kinds of turnarounds.

# Fills

Most 12-bar blues songs consist of three lines of singing: the first line is sung, then repeated, followed by a third line which rhymes with the other two. Each line has approximately the same number of beats. Take a look at *Matchbox Blues* (page 7) and see how the singing fits into a typical 12-bar blues song.

(Up) on the river, Mama, walk down by the sea._____ Up on the river,_____ walk down by the sea._____ I got those tad-poles and minnows all in over me._____

Notice that there are "holes" in the singing where the guitar usually provides an "answer" in the form of a blues fill or riff. Here are some typical fills that you can practice in different keys. With slight variation, these fills can be used as turnarounds.